GUESS

Copyright © 2022 Kim Hamman
All rights reserved
First Edition

PAGE PUBLISHING
Conneaut Lake, PA

First originally published by Page Publishing 2022

ISBN 978-1-6624-7207-7 (pbk)
ISBN 978-1-6624-7208-4 (digital)

Printed in the United States of America

GUESS

Kim Hamman

1

Side by side they look to the sky
They can see far; they can see near
They are so very close to your ear

Blue, green, brown—they see the ground
They see shapes and colors or look at each other

They can blink or even wink
Side by side they look to the sky

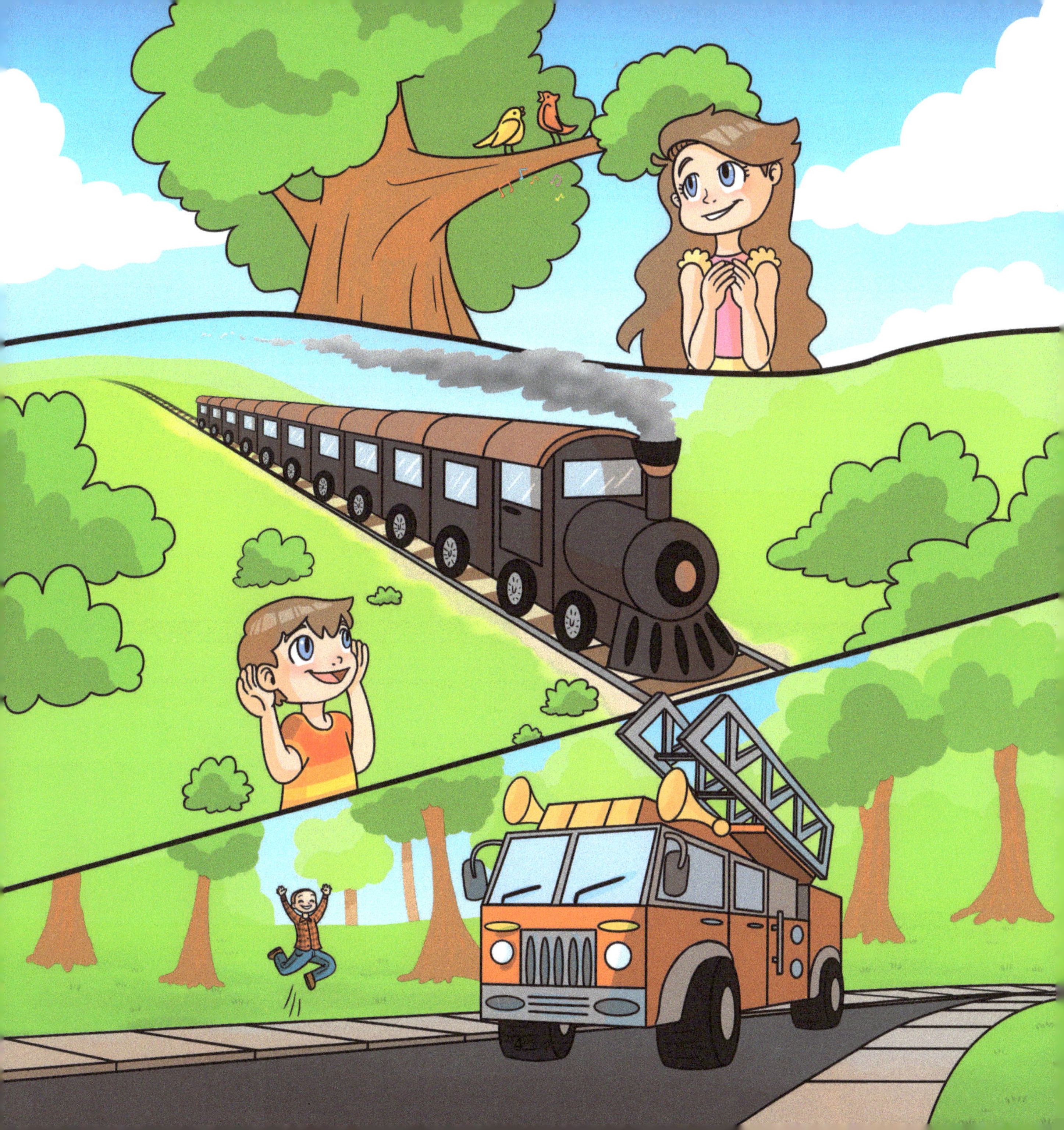

There's two on either side of you
Can you hear? They are near

It can be silent; it can be loud
They can hear any sound
There's two on either side of you

6

There are two on the side of you
They help you swim or climb a limb

They can spin your friends around or keep
you from falling on the ground
There are two on either side of you

Two by two they're as long as you
They can be small or very tall
They have a knee to help you climb a tree

They can skip or do a flip
Two by two they're as long as you

9

Two by two they come in a shoe
They move you around, and their friends can be clowns

They can walk in the park or run and have some fun
Two by two, they come in a shoe

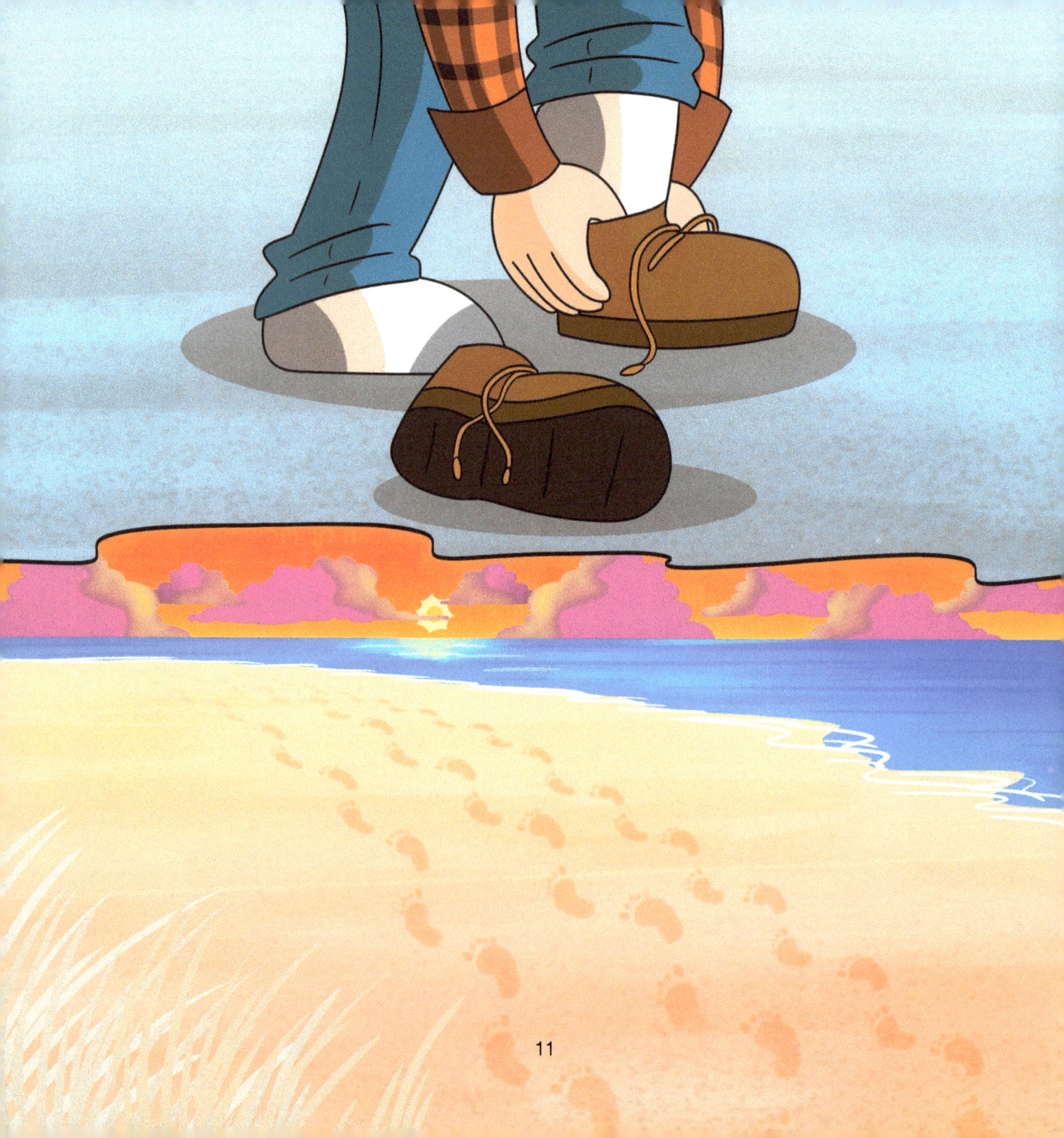

If I'm tall or if I'm small
If I'm big or as little as a twig

I am me, and let me be, and you
are you; lets be friends too

CPSIA information can be obtained
at www.ICGtesting.com
Printed in the USA
BVHW011647220223
659018BV00027B/613